I BELIEVE
IN THE
HOLY SPIRIT

I BELIEVE
IN THE
HOLY SPIRIT

———•———

Ernest F. Scott

ABINGDON PRESS
New York • Nashville

I BELIEVE IN THE HOLY SPIRIT

Copyright © MCMLVIII by Abingdon Press

Library of Congress Catalog Card Number: 58-9524

B

SET UP, PRINTED, AND BOUND BY THE
PARTHENON   PRESS,   AT NASHVILLE
TENNESSEE, UNITED STATES OF AMERICA

CONTENTS

CHAPTER ONE

WHAT WE MEAN BY THE SPIRIT

"I BELIEVE IN THE HOLY SPIRIT." OF ALL THE ARTICLES of the creed this may seem to us the most vague and doubtful. We know what we mean when we declare our faith in God, in Jesus Christ, in the Church, in the future life. But what is the Holy Spirit? To be sure, it is often mentioned in the Bible, and we are willing to believe in it. Yet we believe in it much as we do in the laws of astronomy. We do not pretend to understand those laws; in our everyday living we never think about them. In the same way we feel that we can leave the Spirit out of our religion. But the truth is that nothing is so essential in religion as the Spirit.

Primitive man felt the Spirit

Belief in the Spirit is the very root out of which religion has grown. Long before they worshiped God, men stood in awe of the Spirit. They believed in it because they knew it as a fact in their own experience.

We are wont to think that early man looked out on the world with a sense of wonder we moderns have lost. We suppose that he looked on the glories of nature and the mysteries of man's life as things that were new and marvel-

7

ous. And we suppose that these things are so familiar and common to us that we take them for granted. But the truth is just the other way around. We, with our fuller knowledge, are the ones who have grown alive to the wonder of quite ordinary things. Early man, like the savage today, accepted the world as he found it. Things that were always happening did not seem in any way remarkable to him.

The primitive man's sense of mystery was awakened only by what was contrary to the normal course of nature. The sun was darkened sometimes at midday; accidents took place without any apparent cause; a man became strangely affected in mind or body. Some unknown force must cause these extraordinary things. It was present in the world and came into action from time to time. Often it brought calamity. Sometimes it would go into a man and make him able to do things that seemed utterly beyond his strength. For the earliest men the chief aim of religion was to cope with this disturbing force in nature and human life. What it was they could not tell, but they could not doubt it was real. They supposed certain objects could control it. They devised charms and ceremonies to turn it away or to win it over to their side.

Religion began with this sense of a power outside the visible world. Before they had any name for God, men were aware in a crude and childish way of what we now call the Spirit.

The Hebrews called it the Spirit of God

Primitive man's idea of the Spirit passed over into Hebrew religion. We hear much in the Old Testament of the *ruach*. This word means literally a motion of the air, a gentle wind. The Greeks translated it by their word for "breath," and the Romans called it *spiritus,* which means the same. We can thus guess at the idea in the minds of those ancient men. They were aware of a mysterious power breaking in on the ordinary course of things. They imagined it as moving here and there like a little gust of wind on a calm day. They could not tell what it was or how it was set in motion. They only knew that now and then, quite suddenly, there was a breath that touched them.

We can make out a time in the religion of the early Hebrews when they thought of the Spirit as separate from God. God was the ruler of the world; but there was also this other power, hovering about in the air and interfering sometimes with God's designs. They soon left this idea behind, as their belief in the one God became firmer and clearer. They did not doubt the existence of the Spirit, but they now saw it as the Spirit of God. It was the Holy Spirit, sent forth by God to carry out his purposes.

As yet, they did not connect it with moral ideas. All acts that seemed extraordinary they set down to the Spirit. The Spirit came on Samson, and he tore a lion in pieces. It gave Joseph insight into the meaning of a dream. It helped David to meet one crisis and another in his stormy life. Sometimes they said the Spirit even caused evil things. God planned the downfall of Saul and sent the Spirit on him to drive him mad. God doomed an army to destruction, and the Spirit lured its leaders on with false counsels.

A number of hints in the earlier Old Testament records show that people had as yet no clear beliefs about the nature of the Spirit. They indeed looked on it as the Spirit of God, but they made it account for everything, good or bad, that they could not otherwise explain.

The prophets declared the Spirit is righteous

The great prophets lifted the belief about the Spirit to a different level altogether. It fell to their lot to develop that sense of the righteousness of God that had always lain at the heart of Hebrew religion. They took over the old idea that God did all mysterious things by means of his Spirit, but they brought it into harmony with their own faith that he always does what is right. They gave up the old idea of a nameless power that wandered about like the wind and caused men to do extraordinary things.

The Spirit, as they knew it, was in a real sense the Spirit of the Lord. Its one duty was to bring God's will to pass, and all its action had to be understood in the light of his purpose. The Spirit sent by him was therefore a moral energy, working for moral ends. They assumed that man in himself was a creature of earth who with all his striving could not know and obey God's will. Man must receive from God the wisdom and strength which were lacking to him. "Not by might, nor by power, but by my Spirit, saith the Lord."

The prophets felt the Spirit within them

The prophets thought of their own gift as bestowed on them by the Spirit. In making their pronouncements they said, in effect, "The Spirit of the Lord came upon me," and in that confidence they spoke in the name of God. Perhaps we can take this formula of the prophets in a literal and almost physical sense. We know that in early times there were men in Israel who claimed they could see into the future and who made their forecasts while in a trance.

In the East today the dancing dervishes work themselves into wild excitement and so describe the visions that pass before their eyes. The Delphic prophetess in ancient Greece sat over a sulphur well which gave off fumes that half intoxicated her. We are familiar today with hypnotists and spiritualists who go into trances in order to pry into hidden things. Ancient people knew these practices well. At first they connected prophecy with a peculiar state of mind and body. They believed this state came about when the Spirit took hold of a man's personality. It is possible that Amos and Isaiah and their successors spoke of things they seemed actually to see and hear while they were in a trance.

There is all the difference in the world, though, between

11

the fit of a madman and the ecstasy of a saint or poet. Handel told his friends that when he composed the "Hallelujah Chorus," he could hear angels singing, and he only wrote down the music he was listening to. Tennyson wrote his poem "Crossing the Bar" almost without knowing it. The words came to him, he said, all in a moment. He never could be sure that they were his.

Perhaps the greatest utterances have to come from some power beyond a man. He cannot arrive at them by any effort of his own mind. They need to rise of their own accord when he is caught up out of himself and is in touch with some higher world. The Old Testament prophets were not men who were half crazy, like the wandering soothsayers who had gone before them. Their minds were far clearer than those of other men. They were trained to express themselves in noble language. Yet they felt that what they said had been given them almost without their knowledge. The Spirit of the Lord had come upon them.

All men will someday share the Spirit

Thus the prophets thought of the Spirit as the means of communication between God and man. When God had a truth to reveal, he used the Spirit as his agent, breathing it into some chosen man who was fitted to receive it. The Spirit conveyed the mind of God, and so it was present in every true thought, every higher desire and impulse.

By possessing it men had their natures changed, brought into sympathy with God.

The prophet Joel looks forward to a time when all men and women, even the humblest, will share in the Spirit. Hitherto it has been given only at rare moments to seers and heroes. But "it shall come to pass afterward, that I will pour out my Spirit upon all flesh; and your sons and your daughters shall prophesy, your old men shall dream dreams, your young men shall see visions: and also upon the servants and upon the handmaids in those days will I pour out my Spirit." Some of the greater prophets connect the hope of the Messiah with this coming of the Spirit. Through the Messiah, God will finally carry out his purpose, and therefore the Spirit will rest on him in the fullest measure—"the Spirit of wisdom and understanding, the Spirit of counsel and might, the Spirit of knowledge and of the fear of the Lord." Through the Messiah, God will give the Spirit to his people as their lasting possession.

The Spirit imparts God's life-giving power

God reveals his will through his Spirit. Through the Spirit also he communicates his life-giving power. In a verse that stands at the very beginning of the Bible, we learn how God created the world out of chaos: "The earth was without form, and void; . . . and the Spirit of God moved upon the face of the waters." The Hebrew word which is translated "moved" means literally "brooded," and possibly this is the reason people came to picture the Spirit as a dove—though the idea may be simply that of gentle motion. Whatever we make of details in the creation story, men were thinking of the Spirit as a life-giving power. Nothing existed but a dead mass of matter. The breath of God came into it and produced life and order.

The same idea meets us repeatedly in the Old Testament: "By his Spirit he hath garnished the heavens." "Thou sendest forth thy Spirit, they are created: and thou renewest the face of the earth." "There is a Spirit in man: and the inspiration of the Almighty giveth them understanding." God is the living One, and he gives life to his creatures by touching them with his Spirit. By means of it he gives to men a higher kind of life, so they become different from the beasts that die. This idea was already hinted at in the Old Testament and is fully unfolded in the New.

Jesus lived by the Spirit

Between the Old Testament prophets and Jesus there lies a period of about three centuries, during which the Hebrew religion went through many changes. These changes were due to many causes, but most of all to putting the Law in first place. Men read in the Scriptures how God had given all the rules of the Law to Moses, and they began to suppose the whole service of God lay in following those rules. As a result they thought of the Spirit less

14

and less, as men always do when religion becomes a matter of routine to them. They assumed God had revealed all his will in the Law, and by keeping it faithfully men would share in the divine life. In one of the later psalms, perhaps the latest of all, the writer complains: "There is no more any prophet." All was now formal and mechanical. No longer were there prophets who brought fresh messages from God. Instead there were only priests who performed the ceremonies of the Law and rabbis who expounded its meaning.

When Jesus came, men felt again the living presence of the Spirit. At the beginning of his ministry, when he was called on to speak in the synagogue of Nazareth, he read out a passage in Isaiah, "The Spirit of the Lord is upon me." Then he declared, "This day this scripture is fulfilled in your ears." It is true that in his teaching, as recorded in the first three Gospels, he said little about the Spirit. He did not need to speak of it, since it showed in all he said and did. We take the air for granted because we are breathing it every moment; for Jesus the Spirit was like the air he lived by. It guided him in all his acts; it inspired his prayers. In everything he taught, he was declaring the mind of the Spirit.

In one remarkable saying Jesus spoke of the Spirit plainly, but only because his enemies had said he did not possess it. They had to admit he did wonderful things, but they saw in this a proof that he was in collusion with the devil. In the Middle Ages people made the same charge against Joan of Arc and against the inventor of the printing press. There are people who make it still, in more modern language, against those who help them most. They will not believe that anyone does a noble act except from some low motive and by wicked means. Jesus pointed out that all his work was for the good of man and that man's enemy would never fight against himself. Only the Holy Spirit could give power to heal the sick and bring peace and freedom and happiness. Then he went on to say that all other sins will be forgiven, but for him who slanders the Holy Spirit there can be no forgiveness in this world or the next. (See Matt. 12:31-32.)

This saying on the sin that cannot be forgiven has puzzled many people and sometimes has caused acute misery. John Bunyan tells us that for several years as a young man he lived in utter despair because once in a rash moment he had spoken a blasphemy against the Holy Spirit. He felt that henceforth he was shut off from all mercy, that he had committed the one sin that could not be forgiven.

But it is not hard to understand what Jesus meant. He declares there can be no hope for those who call good evil, who mock and slander a work that is clearly of God. Their moral instincts have become twisted. The conscience that might have drawn them to repentance and a better life has been paralyzed. Blindness to the Holy Spirit is indeed the sin that cannot be forgiven.

The apostles received power from the Spirit

After the death and resurrection of Jesus his disciples were fully awakened to the meaning of his life and his Cross. They realized that through him the Spirit was now working mightily. The days of mechanical religion were now over. God was speaking to men and filling them with a new life.

The Church came into being through this consciousness that the Spirit had come. The book of Acts tells us this consciousness burst on the disciples when they were met together on the day of Pentecost, seven weeks after the Passover on which Jesus had died. They suddenly heard a sound like a rushing wind—and at once they felt a strange new power, most notably a new kind of speech. We can only guess now, after so long a time, as to the exact nature of this "speaking with tongues" that was practiced in the early Church. But whatever it was, it was proof to the disciples of something given them that they had never known before. An energy was in them, as when a machine lying idle is joined up with the electric current. What was this energy? They remembered, we are told, the prophecy of Joel about the coming of the Spirit in the latter days. The promised time had now arrived, they thought. The power they now felt was the Spirit of God within them.

It was on the day of Pentecost that Jesus' followers had their first experience of the Spirit. This gave rise to a belief that had a great influence on later Christian thought. The

Spirit had come a short time after Jesus had departed, so his followers decided Jesus had sent it after his return to heaven to make up for his own absence. He was no longer visible to his people; he could not personally direct and help them as he had hitherto done. But he had sent the Spirit to act for him. He was like a dear friend who has moved to a distant country but still sends constant messages to those he has left behind him. So through the Spirit the people of Jesus were kept in fellowship with him. This thought finds expression in many beautiful passages of the Gospel of John: "I will pray the Father, and he shall give you another Comforter . . . . I will not leave you comfortless: I will come to you." "The Comforter, which is the Holy Ghost, whom the Father will send in my name, he shall teach you all things."

It may be well to note that the word "Comforter" has changed its meaning since the Bible was translated into English three centuries ago. It now suggests one who offers consolation, but it is taken from the Latin *confortare,* which means "make strong." This meaning is still kept in the phrase "give comfort to the enemy," which does not mean that you cheer him up, but that you actively support him. This is certainly what the word means in the Gospel. The Spirit is described as a divine power which sustains us when we are weak, which gives courage and energy and helps us do things that seem utterly beyond us. Jesus did all that for his disciples when he was still with them, and he now sends the Spirit to take his place. He has

18

departed from our sight, but in his Spirit he is with us still.

Paul gave us our full idea of the Spirit

It was Paul who first grasped the idea of the Spirit in its full significance. Christians before him had felt a new power brought them by their faith, but they had not reflected on what it did or how it acted. Paul took up the belief in the Spirit as he found it in the early Church and placed it at the very center of his teaching. Whatever subject he writes about, whether it is the sublimest truth or some trivial point of daily duty, he always comes back to the Spirit. In a textbook of science we never get away from the principle of cause and effect. Everything in the material world must conform to it. In much the same manner Paul relates everything in the Christian life to the action of the Spirit.

In three ways Paul goes beyond the idea of the Spirit which earlier men held. Let us examine these three ways in which he carried the idea of the Spirit forward.

The Spirit acts in our everyday life

For one thing, Paul sees the Spirit at work in man's life as a whole when man places his life under the rule of Christ. Those before him had recognized the Spirit only in strange events—in rare gifts like speaking with tongues or performing miracles. Paul does not deny what these earlier men said: we must understand that mysterious

19

things happen because a higher power breaks in on the ordinary course of nature. He grants that some men have exceptional gifts, that in some rare moods they are lifted above themselves, by the operation of the Spirit within them. He tells, for instance, that he himself was thrice caught up into the third heaven and heard things it was not lawful for man to utter. This state of ecstasy he credits to the Spirit. So while Paul agrees with the earlier Christians—while he grants the value of these high moments of life—he goes beyond that. He is always trying to show that the Spirit reveals itself in our everyday acts.

In one place Paul lists the various forms of work that he thinks of as coming from the Spirit. He includes among them teaching, leadership, hospitality, business administration. God made men different, and each one has his special capacity. If you are a great thinker or saint or poet, you may claim to possess the Spirit. But you may claim the Spirit just as truly if you are faithful in your daily calling, whatever it may be.

Paul thus goes beyond the old idea that the Spirit shows itself only in abnormal action. He says it occupies itself with the whole of life. In everything a man does, he may have the Spirit helping him.

The Spirit is our abiding possession

The second way Paul goes beyond the old idea of the Spirit is that he thinks the Spirit is an abiding possession. According to the old idea the Spirit came rarely and then only for a moment. In the midst of his common life a man was visited with this divine power and did his marvelous deed. Then the Spirit left him, and he sank again into his ordinary self. Paul agrees there are times when the Spirit uplifts us, and such times are of priceless value. But he goes beyond this earlier idea. He holds that the power which thus springs into action, like a volcano, is always present. We receive the Spirit in the act by which we put our faith in Christ. We may count on its staying with us, even when we are not aware of it. Our life from then on is "life in the Spirit," for this other power has become one with our own will and disposition.

Thackeray describes a man he admired walking home one night through the streets of London. "I do not know what he was thinking of," Thackeray says, "but I am sure that he had kind and honorable thoughts, for they were always with him." We have all known people we could say that about. We feel that we could never surprise them in any unworthy thought or act. They may be concerned for the moment with some quite trifling thing, but their minds are set immovably on what is good.

This is "life in the Spirit." A higher power has entered into the old nature. It has come not as a passing impulse but as a principle that now governs the will. It may show itself from time to time in some grand act of courage or wisdom or self-sacrifice, but it does not have to appear this way. The highest kind of life is that in which the Spirit does not flash and disappear, but shines always with a steady light. This is a new understanding of the Spirit which Paul gave to us. The Spirit does not pay brief visits to man; it lives with him always.

The Spirit does Christ's work in us

The third way in which Paul goes beyond earlier ideas of the Spirit is that he thinks of the Spirit as coming to us to do the work of Christ within us. In early times, as I have said, men thought of the Spirit merely as the cause of actions that were outside the range of common experience. Samson was by no means a man to admire. But because he could carry the gates of a city on his shoulders, the early men thought of him as a man moved by the Spirit. All through the Old Testament we find the idea that marvelous things of any kind were due to the Spirit. Most of the early Christians had the same belief.

Paul tells the Christians of Corinth that their chief ambition has been to "speak with tongues," to know more than other men, to do deeds that would look like miracles. If they could do things like this, they assumed, men would know beyond doubt that they had received the Spirit. So Paul tries to impress on them that these displays mean little or nothing. The Spirit comes from God, he says, and the one sign of its presence is that it gives men the power to do the will of God as Christ revealed it. All acts that help on the cause of Christ, in a man's own life or in the world at large, are made possible by the Spirit. And the Spirit is often most active when it does nothing that seems out of the common.

With this thought in his mind Paul wrote his most famous and beautiful chapter, the thirteenth chapter of First Corinthians, in praise of love. He has been speaking of gifts of the Spirit and has discussed those gifts that men wish for most. All of these gifts, he says, have their place when they are used for a right purpose. Then he goes on, "Yet shew I unto you a more excellent way." Then through all the beautiful thirteenth chapter he explains that the greatest gift of the Spirit is love. All the other gifts are secondary. They are worth while only for a time. The Spirit is most truly present within us when it creates in us that disposition of love which was Christ's. The other things all pass away, but "faith, hope, love abide, these three; but the greatest of these is love."

Paul contrasts the Spirit with what he calls the "flesh" and declares that the two are hostile to each other. "They that are in the flesh cannot please God." "The mind of the flesh is death." We would naturally suppose that by the "flesh" Paul means the body. Because they took it to mean that, the hermits of old made it their aim to starve and torment their bodies. In this way they hoped to change themselves into purely spiritual men. But this is certainly not Paul's meaning.

Paul knows that bodily health is necessary to all kinds of useful action and that proper care of the body is in this respect a religious duty. When he speaks of the "flesh," he is thinking in a general way of our lower nature. For him the "flesh" includes all the passions and motives that belong to us merely as animals. When our mind is set wholly on these lower interests—on what we eat and drink, on the wealth and power that secure us a good position in the world, on our personal safety and the applause of our fellow men—then we are living after the flesh and forgetting the true purpose of life.

When Paul speaks of the "flesh," then, he means what we now call materialism. He says that to live solely for material ends is death. And surely he is right. When we know of nothing in the world that we cannot value in terms of money, then we are not really alive. We have completely missed the very things for which life was given us.

So Paul believes that the Spirit comes to us to make us aware of a higher world. In that world the things that count are all of a different kind from those which we can see and handle. In our true being we belong to that other world. The Spirit awakens love and goodness and worship in us so that we may become our true selves.

Paul tells us, therefore, that the aim of the Christian life is to produce the "fruits of the Spirit." This phrase, which he uses again and again, says a great deal. It suggests, for one thing, that the ability to do right actions has to be sown in us. Our field does not produce a harvest when we leave it to itself. We have to plant seed in it, brought perhaps from a great distance. Then the soil and the seed work together to bear a harvest. So in our lives we must do our own part, but our efforts go for nothing unless the Spirit has given us the seed—the impulse toward that which is good and just and lovely. When the seed is there, the harvest will appear in due time of its own accord—if we protect the seed and see that it is not destroyed.

In the time of Paul people thought that good lives had to be made by some process from outside the person. The Jews had their elaborate system of the Law, which was supposed to make everyone righteous who carefully followed it. Every pagan country had its code of moral rules. In our own time many people believe that by new methods of education and new social arrangements we can create a world of men and women who will all do what is right.

Paul held that right action is like fruit that comes naturally when the seed is planted in the proper soil—and otherwise will not come at all. We cannot serve God by any set rules. We need his Holy Spirit in our hearts, and when it is planted there, it will spring up of its own accord and bring forth fruit.

CHAPTER TWO

WHAT THE SPIRIT DOES

WE HAVE CONSIDERED HOW THE BELIEF IN THE HOLY Spirit arose and how it passed through a long development before it finally became one of the chief elements in the Christian faith. Almost from the beginning men had the idea of a mysterious power that entered at times into the life they knew. They thought of it at first as something like wind or lightning, but as time went on, they saw more deeply into its nature. They learned to connect it with truth and love and holiness. Yet the earliest man who ever spoke of this power was dimly conscious of one thing: he felt there was another world which breaks at times into this one and makes everything different.

Men have always known the Spirit as a fact

We should remember that from the very beginning men believed in the Spirit because they knew it as a fact. We are wont to dismiss most things in primitive religion as just fancies or superstitions. In those long-ago times men knew very little about the world. They worshiped many gods and had traditions about who the gods were and what they had done. They practiced many ceremonies, which were often very elaborate, and believed that in this way they pleased the gods. But we know now that those gods never existed and that all the efforts to win their favor were thrown away. So we think of early religion as nothing more than myth and delusion, of no value to anyone but the psychologist and the student of the past. But the belief in the Spirit is on a different footing. It arose from a real experience and one that meets us still. We are conscious of moods and impulses we cannot account for. As we pass through this earthly life, we find ourselves in contact with another order of things. And from the beginning men have felt the same.

Here, then, we have a belief that links the present with the most distant times we know of. This belief has held its own because it is grounded in a fact that has always been apparent. There is a power we cannot explain, and yet it is as real as any other.

Ever and again in the midst of a quite ordinary life a man is seized with a great enthusiasm. He is going about some daily task when a thought flashes in upon him. He cannot tell where it comes from, but it makes him look at all things in a different way. In a time of crisis or difficulty, when he is giving up in despair, he feels suddenly that he has become strong. He is able to bear up and overcome his troubles.

What is this power that is other than our own? We cannot explain it any more than men could thousands of years ago. We can only say, as they did, that something

27

is breathed in upon us out of another world. That something gives us strength and understanding.

When we say, "I believe in the Holy Spirit," we are not agreeing to some vague church doctrine that means nothing to us personally. It is the one declaration we can vouch for out of our own experience. We believe in it because again and again it has actually come to us. We have felt it just as surely as we would feel the touch of a friend's hand.

Men have always known the Spirit as a power

We must notice, too, that men have always understood the Spirit as an energy. The New Testament writers hardly ever mention it without some reference to power. "The power of the Spirit." "Power from on high." These are phrases they constantly repeat. It is much the same in the Old Testament and as far back as we can go.

The existence of the Spirit was a fact. It was also a fact that the Spirit showed itself in the work it did. It is indeed strange that men should give the Spirit credit for the physical strength of Samson, but this at least shows how their minds were running even in those early times. They knew the Spirit was an energy. They might not analyze the way it worked, but they knew that when it entered into a man, he was made strong. In later days people realized that true strength was not physical but intellectual and moral. This also was connected with the Spirit. Men are weak in themselves, but this power from above enters into them and makes them able to do great things.

Here, too, we must remember this is not just an old superstition. Men knew from experience that at times those who seemed quite helpless received a new energy. They could not explain this by natural causes. They could explain it only as the power of the Spirit. That is how men felt in far-off ages and how we still feel when the same miracle happens today.

The Spirit, then, is a power, given us from above, which comes to the aid of our human weakness. No one can discover exactly what it is, but the name that describes it best is the one given to it by John—the "Comforter," the "Helper."

There are many ways in which the Spirit gives its power. The New Testament writers, especially Paul and John, have much to say on this subject. And what they say has been proved in the lives of men during all the centuries that followed. Most of us can prove its truth from things that have happened to us. We know the Spirit is real because we have seen it working in our own lives and in those around us.

We call one of the New Testament books the Acts of the Apostles, but this title was chosen for it after the book was written and does not properly define it. We ought rather to call it the Acts of the Spirit, for the whole aim of the author is to show that it was not the apostles themselves who acted. At the close of each section of his history he pauses and says, in varying words, that all this was plainly done in the might of the Spirit. The apostles had set themselves to an impossible task, and yet they succeeded in doing it. They knew they could do nothing by their own strength, but they felt that the Spirit was with them. By this divine help they could face their enemies. They could bear up under persecution and carry their message victoriously from land to land.

So we can trace the hand of the Spirit in all history since then. Many writers today take pleasure in belittling our great men. They like to show that in most ways these men were quite ordinary and far from worthy of the pedestals we have set them on. This view of them is no doubt largely true. But the fact remains that huge responsibilities were laid on them, and with all their faults they proved equal to their task. They must have been the instruments used by a power beyond their own, and the greatest of these men have always been the first to admit that this was true.

Little credit is due to men themselves for the marvelous things they have done, far less credit than we ever suppose. The greatness of a man consists in nothing else than this: he is able to wait humbly for the strength that comes to him through the Spirit.

The Spirit makes men free

The New Testament writers speak often of the effects this higher energy has on man's nature. For one thing it gives him freedom. Paul especially stresses this side of the work of the Spirit. He knows he has at last become a free man. He rejoices in his liberty, as a prisoner does when he first steps out into the open air.

Paul thinks chiefly of his freedom from the Law. All his life previously he has lived under this system of the Law, which never allowed a man to act for himself but hedged him about with countless rules and restrictions. Now he is free of this tyranny of the Law, for the Spirit has come upon him, and he has only to follow its direction. In every matter concerning the Law he is free to use his own judgment and will.

This escape from the Law that the Spirit won for him brought with it many other kinds of freedom. He can feel now that he is not a slave to other men, or to old traditions, or to any outward force that tries to rule him. "The Spirit," he says, "bears witness to our spirits that we are children of God." He means there is something divine in us that is awakened by the Spirit and responds to it. We did not know before that we were anything more than creatures of this earth, and as such we were content with any slavery that men might impose on us. Now we are made to realize that we are children of God. We are responsible to God alone.

We are always talking of freedom and boasting that we live in a free country, but very few people ever ask themselves what freedom is. We associate it with some kind of government or with the right to run our own lives without interference from nagging laws and overseers. These things, however, are only by-products of freedom; we may enjoy them without having freedom itself. Indeed we often find that the more security men gain, the less they are free. They learn to cling timidly to outward supports. They become unable to think and act for themselves even in the smallest matters.

Freedom is not a matter of the things around us; it is something in our souls. We need to feel that we are *ourselves*. We must feel that we have a higher nature that cannot be controlled by anything in this world. This sense that we belong to God, and to him alone, must somehow be stirred in us before we can be free. This is the work of the Spirit.

It is a simple fact that every struggle for freedom has begun with an enthusiasm, rising at first in the hearts of a few and then spread by them to the many. No appeal to their worldly interests will ever rouse men out of their slavery. Something within them must be set in motion. They must realize they have souls of their own. They must know that if they sell themselves to other men, they are false to the God who made them.

It is the Spirit that brings us the desire for freedom and also brings us the strength to win it. This is one of the facts that stand out in all the records of history. Men never win freedom without a long and painful struggle. In order to endure that struggle, men must be supported by a power not their own. In the face of all calamity they must look to God, who encourages and sustains them by his Spirit in their hearts.

The Spirit reveals God to men

The work of the Spirit also takes another form. It appears in the Old Testament as the gift bestowed on the prophets. The Spirit of the Lord came upon them, and they could see into the future. They were given insight into the ways of God. They looked forward to the Messiah, who would understand all things. They foretold a time when not only the chosen prophets but all God's people, even the humblest, would possess the Spirit.

This idea of the Spirit as the source of all revelation meets us constantly in the New Testament. We are told over and over again that men by themselves cannot know the mind of God. Human wisdom can make wonderful discoveries, but it cannot go beyond a certain point. If we are ever to know the highest things, they must be revealed to us by God himself.

Jesus tells us that such things are hidden, most often, from the wise and prudent. Strangely enough, the very faculties we pride ourselves on—our five senses, which help us to learn all other things—prove an actual hindrance when we try to understand these higher things. God himself must give us understanding; all he asks of us is the trustful, receptive heart.

All the New Testament teachers repeat this thought of Jesus in many different ways. We could almost say that this thought contains the whole substance of their message. God has offered to reveal himself, and he does this through his Spirit. On our part we must have the faith that can respond to it.

The Spirit speaks directly to every man

We have seen that the Spirit is the source of revelation. Here the New Testament lays stress on a fact that came to be strangely overlooked in later days. That fact is this: the Spirit comes directly to every believer. Paul impresses on his followers that they must not depend on any human teacher, since the truth is given to each man individually by the Spirit, and what he believes only on the word of some other man is not his own faith. Paul complains that the Christians at Corinth are dividing themselves into groups, each calling itself by the name of some outstanding leader and claiming that only his account of the gospel is the right one. Paul himself is one of the leaders who are thus honored, but he will have none of it. He says to the men of Corinth, "You must not listen to me but to the Spirit, for the truth which comes to you at second hand is not really yours and will avail you nothing." The New Testament writers all demand this personal response to the voice of the Spirit.

Yet a time came when early Christians felt this teaching was dangerous. They asked how the Church could hold together if each of its members was allowed to interpret the message in his own way. So they decided that God had sent the Spirit to the *Church as a whole*. The Spirit spoke only through the Church's duly ordained leaders. All members of the Church must believe the gospel as these men taught it. To differ from them in any way was to sin against the Spirit. Now this view has always been held by the Roman Catholic Church, and most other churches believe it also to a lesser degree. But it is a complete turning around of the New Testament teaching.

For Paul the Spirit meant liberty. He declared that all Christians have received the Spirit and that no man can dictate to others what they must believe. Your opinions may not be the same as mine; but if you are convinced that what you believe has been taught you by the Spirit, then you must hold the truth in your own way and in no other.

We cannot doubt that the Church has done itself a great deal of harm by setting itself up in place of the Spirit. Often it has cast out and persecuted the men who would have served it best. It has turned conscientious men into hypocrites—as they try to hold beliefs of the Church that in their hearts they do not feel to be true. The New Testament teaching is always that we must obey God and not man. He reveals himself to each one of us by his Spirit; where it leads us, we must follow. Thus the Spirit speaks to each man individually.

The Spirit lets each man know a living Christ

Now we come to a second element in the New Testament teaching that was strangely forgotten by the later

Church. The New Testament teachers stressed the fact that the Spirit is the source of a living revelation. When Paul came forward as an apostle, many of the earlier disciples doubted him. They said he had not known Jesus personally, and therefore he could not report Jesus' message like those who heard it with their own ears.

Paul's answer was that he knew Christ just as truly as the others, for Christ had risen and was still speaking through the Spirit. All who had received the Spirit were in direct fellowship with Christ. They might not declare his message exactly as it had come to the first disciples, but it was still the authentic message. Paul said if we listen to the Spirit, we hear Christ speaking—even though he doesn't simply repeat what he has said before.

Paul therefore deals with many questions Jesus himself had never touched on. He tells his followers how to meet difficulties which face them in Gentile cities—cities Jesus had never heard of. He puts the gospel into new words and new forms of thought. He never doubts this is what Christ says. Since Christ is living still, he does not merely say the old things over again. He reveals new truth through his Spirit and tells us what he demands of us here in the present.

John develops this idea of a living revelation more fully; indeed his whole Gospel may be said to turn on it. John records what Jesus did on earth, but he tries to show us that this was only the beginning of a work that is still going on. "The water that I shall give him shall be in him a well of water." Not a stagnant pool but a well, always springing up afresh. So at the Last Supper, Jesus speaks of the Spirit he will send after his departure. In his life on earth he had brought a revelation. Now the Spirit will continue it and unfold it. "I have yet many things to say unto you, but ye cannot bear them now." In the time to come Jesus will gradually bring these other things to light. New generations will live under new conditions. They will have knowledge the first disciples lacked, and they will understand the message in a new and larger way.

So John thinks of Christianity as a revelation that is ever renewing itself. It is always responding to the world's changing needs and taking into itself fresh elements, but still it is the revelation which Jesus gave. "The Spirit will take the things that are mine and will disclose them unto you."

Men are to rely on the Spirit as they have relied on Christ himself, and the Spirit will guide them "unto all truth." This for John is the special work of the Spirit—it keeps renewing the message and making it real under all changing conditions. It brings it home to men in the form that each new age can best understand.

This, then, is an idea that has never found its right place in the teaching of the Church. From a very early time church leaders tried to put every Christian practice and belief in a fixed form. They drew up creeds that were never to be changed in any way. They wrote rules of worship and allowed no changes in them.

From time to time there were men who discovered some new truth in the Christian message, but they were not allowed a hearing. Great changes took place in the world of thought or action, and thinking men tried to make religion keep step with them, but this was sternly forbidden. Now and then, as in the time of the Reformation, Christian men have rebelled against these conditions. The living Spirit has forced its way through the ice.

But in the main the old idea has stayed with us: all change is dangerous, and religion will lose itself if it tries to strike out on any new road. This attitude of mind is just the reverse of what the New Testament teachers believed. They believed in the Holy Spirit. They were confident that by means of it Christ was ever renewing his message. He was ever speaking to each generation in its own language.

The Spirit unites men in common purpose

The Spirit brings with it a sense of freedom. It enables men to feel they must not be held down by forms and traditions or by the opinions of other men. But while it gives them this personal freedom, it also gathers them into a community.

The Church came into being when a group of separate men, gathered together, realized they had all received the Spirit. So the New Testament writers think of the Spirit as the great bond of Christian union. Possessing the Spirit in common, the believers are made aware that they have the same interests and are all working toward the same ends.

Why is it that the same power that assures each man that he is a separate individual should also bind men up with one another? Paul answers this question in I Cor. 12, one of the most thought-provoking chapters he ever wrote. He declares that man can never find true unity without difference. He points out that nothing is so clearly one thing as the human body. Yet the body is made up of many members, each with its own special job. No two things could be more different than the eye and the foot. Yet these members are necessary to each other; they are necessary because they are so different. Each member of the body supplies what the other lacks. That is why they are united and can work together.

So long before our day Paul explains a truth that modern scientists now think of as fundamental. *Unity through difference*—that is the law which holds our universe together. It is also the law of all true society, as we are now learning by hard experience. Men used to take it for granted that if a nation was to be solidly united, the people should be made as much alike as possible. They must be forced to think in the same way about everything. They must do the same things. They must have the same identical character. Leaders of this system set up methods of drill and education that were intended to stamp out all individuality. They wanted to mold millions of people after one given pattern.

Some nations still follow this system, but it is false in its very nature. A community of human beings is not like a block of sandstone, made up of particles which are all the same and need only to be crushed together. Each man and woman is different from the rest, and these differences must be allowed full play. We get unity, just as the human body does, when each member performs his own special job and all work together in harmony. This is the ideal of a free state. It is proving itself more and more to be the only principle that makes for real union.

Paul insists the Church must be united in this way. Every Christian receives the Spirit as an individual, and this might appear to separate them. The Spirit makes each man aware that he is himself and apart from all the others. It assigns him his own special job in working for the cause of Christ. Perhaps it is a very humble job, which he would like to change for something better. But unity comes to a group when each member does the thing that only he can do. So they all help one another and uphold the common life.

We can easily make a church seem united by denying freedom to the members, but this kind of unity is unity in name only. When people come together only because they are forced together, they will break apart again for the least cause, for secretly they are wishing to do so. The only unity that is worth anything is unity of heart and mind, brought about by the Spirit, which works separately in all the different persons and builds them up into one body of Christ.

So the work of the Spirit takes many forms. Its fruit, says Paul, is love, joy, peace, longsuffering, gentleness, goodness, faith, meekness, temperance. It guides us and strengthens us and gives us understanding. Where the Spirit is, there is liberty. But actually its gifts can be summed up in one statement: it creates a new life. Through his Spirit, God gives us not only the knowledge of himself but also something of his own nature, so that our whole being is transformed. The New Testament teaching deals mainly with this change that the Spirit brings about in the very nature of men.

The Spirit makes men whole

We must never forget that everywhere in the Bible the writers connect the Spirit with power. They make no attempt to explain what it is, for they know it only by what it does. We feel this way about all the greatest things— life, love, poetry, music, beauty. We cannot say exactly what they are. We hear the wind, says John, but we don't know where it comes from or where it goes. So it is with the Spirit. We can tell from what it does that it is a mighty power, but we can explain it only by saying it is breathed into us by God.

In early times people thought of it as some kind of actual substance. A mysterious something was poured into men and worked on their minds and bodies. It changed them into something different from what they were. Even the New Testament writers seem now and then to fall back on this idea. They describe the action of the Spirit almost in physical terms. But their aim is always to convince us that the Spirit is a power from above, which enters into our earthly nature and changes it.

This thought of a life-giving power is impressed on us in different ways. In the Gospels, Jesus appears as the great Healer. Men bring the sick and the disabled to him, and by his touch a new energy enters into them and makes them whole. He heals the soul as well as the body. His word gives sinners and outcasts the power to throw off their evil past.

The New Testament reminds us constantly of this healing brought about by the Spirit. Paul bids the Corinthians take notice of the ruined lives which are all around them. Then he adds, "And such were some of you: but ye are washed, but ye are sanctified, but ye are justified in the name of the Lord Jesus, and by the Spirit of our God." They had been morally diseased, but a divine power has taken hold of them and brought them back to health.

We sometimes describe this healing process as a cleansing. We open the window of a room where there has been sickness, and the fresh air flows in and purifies it. London was stricken by the plague, which left its pollution everywhere. Then a fire swept over the city and burned away all the lurking disease. The Spirit acts in the same way on an evil life. It causes a new power to rush into that life and destroy the very germs of all that was foul and degrading.

There is evidence that early in the second century some groups in the Church dropped the words "Thy kingdom come" from the Lord's Prayer. They used these words instead: "May thy Spirit come upon us and cleanse us." Some scholars argue that this was the original form of the prayer. They say it was written this way in the oldest copies of Luke's Gospel.

We have many reasons for believing that Jesus prayed, "Thy kingdom come," but the other petition agrees fully with his thought. He knew that before men can receive the Kingdom, they must be cleansed inside. The old habits and desires that hold them fettered to this world must be rooted out before they can hope to enter the kingdom of God. This purifying is the work of the Spirit.

The Spirit gives men new life

Along with healing and cleansing, the Spirit brings a sense of uplifting. Those who receive it are conscious of an ardor they never felt before. Something has come into them that makes life worth living, and now they can throw themselves with joy into the hardest task. This has always been the sign of the Spirit that we can see best. It fills a man with enthusiasm. It shakes him out of the ruts of his old life and makes him feel as if he had wings.

The Christians in the earliest days were so moved by the Spirit that they were hardly able to control themselves.

They behaved in the strangest manner, and Paul found it necessary to warn them that strangers coming into their assembly would think they were mad. This is what happens even now in a time of revival. A wild enthusiasm starts up in a crowd of people; sometimes it breaks through all bonds of reason. But this proves at least that a new impulse is at work. Men have felt a rapture. They have been lifted out of themselves. They must have that experience before they will ever arrive at anything great.

So whether it heals or purifies or kindles, the Spirit has this effect of giving us more life. Later New Testament teachers carry this idea out to its full issue. The work of the Spirit is to give life. In their natural state men are not alive, or at least they live only as the animals do, with no sense of anything but the passing moment. The Spirit raises us from the dead. It makes us partakers of that higher life that God has called us to.

This is the truth that John tries to put across when he speaks of the "new birth" or "birth from above," for the word he uses has both of these meanings. We are born into this world with all the faculties that belong to a human creature, but "ye must be born again." We must go through change just as far-reaching as that which brought us here out of nothingness. As yet we are only half born. We are meant to share not only in this earthly life but also in God's own life. For this purpose God breathes his Spirit into us. This thought is a profound and in many ways a very difficult thought, but its main meaning is clear. A new life means a new man altogether. It is not enough that we give up one bad habit and another making ourselves reformed characters as far as we can. We must go through a change at the very center of our being. Our whole purpose and disposition must become different. Only a power not our own can make this change for us.

The basic change sometimes comes through one sudden experience. The Spirit came to Paul this way, and so he thought it always came in this manner. He tells us that the moment we put our faith in Christ, we pass from darkness into light, from death into life, from the world of sin into the world of righteousness.

But we see proof on every side that the action of the Spirit is sometimes so slow that we hardly notice it. The new life arises not from a single convulsion but from silent influences that work together steadily for years. Yet the Spirit brings this about just as surely as if we could point to one moment when we became a new man.

Paul himself allows for a quiet growth in the life of the Spirit. "We all, with open face beholding as in a glass the glory of the Lord, are changed into the same image from glory to glory, even as by the Spirit of the Lord."

CHAPTER THREE

THE SPIRIT'S RELATION TO GOD AND CHRIST

MANY CHRISTIAN PEOPLE, IF YOU ASKED THEM WHAT they mean by the Holy Spirit, would answer at once, "The Holy Spirit is the third Person in the Trinity." We should remember that the early Christians would not have understood this statement. They were deeply aware of the Holy Spirit. They believed that Christ had sent it to take his place after he had departed. They placed their lives completely under its direction. Yet the doctrine of the Trinity, which we now associate it with, arose much later. The New Testament never mentions this doctrine. This, however, does not mean the doctrine is not true. A thing may be very real although we don't understand its nature. Water, for instance, has always been a prime necessity of life, but chemists have only recently discovered how it is composed. That does not mean the formula they have taught us is their own invention. Water is actually composed as the formula says; the chemists have only brought the fact to light. This may be true also of the doctrine of the Trinity, in which the great Christian thinkers stated their beliefs about the nature of the Spirit.

The New Testament idea of the Spirit

The New Testament teachers did not definitely regard the Holy Spirit as a person. To be sure, the early Christian writers sometimes describe it as though they are talking about a person. The Spirit, they say, warns us, comforts us, guides us, speaks to God in our behalf. It knows men's hearts and is grieved by their resistance. But all ancient writers were wont to speak of abstract things in personal terms. They forgot at times that they were using figurative language. We often do the same thing when we speak of war as a monster, of our country as a mother, of peace and happiness as lovely maidens.

The New Testament teachers pick up the idea of the Spirit as they find it in the Old Testament. They think of a divine energy that lays hold of men. They compare it to wind and fire. Paul contrasts it with the flesh; he says the Spirit is a higher element over against the lower element of the flesh. John speaks of "water and the Spirit" as two things that may work together. Even when the writers seem to be describing the Spirit as a person, the basic New Testament idea is always that it is a supernatural force coming into our earthly lives. Sometimes they call it simply the "power of God."

Looking ahead to the doctrine of the Trinity

Thus the New Testament does not speak of the Spirit as a person. Neither does it speak of the threefold nature of God. It assumes, as the Old Testament does, that God is one and that this is the basic truth of religion. Several passages in the New Testament, however, seem to look forward to the later doctrine. One is at the close of Matthew's Gospel: "Go ye, . . . and teach all nations, baptizing them in the name of the Father, and of the Son, and of the Holy Ghost." This verse bears all the signs of having been rewritten after Matthew's time—after the rite of baptism had been set in a fixed pattern. Paul tells us clearly that baptism in the early Church was "in the name of Christ." That was the very purpose of baptism—to assure that the convert should acknowledge Christ as his Master and put his trust in Christ to save him. Except for this one verse in Matthew the New Testament writers always connect baptism with the name of Christ alone.

Another New Testament passage that suggests the doctrine of the Trinity is the benediction most of us know so well. Paul uses a number of benedictions, but the one at the close of Second Corinthians has been widely adopted by the Church: "The grace of the Lord Jesus Christ, and the love of God, and the communion of the Holy Ghost, be with you all." It is strange that while we all know these words so well and use them all the time, yet we cannot be sure what they mean. That phrase at the end, "the communion of the Holy Ghost," can mean three different things: fellowship with the Spirit, imparting of the Spirit, union brought by the Spirit. These meanings are all equally possible and have all found men to support them. But if we think of other things that Paul said, we see that the last meaning is the most probable—union brought by the Spirit.

Paul speaks of the Spirit, as we have seen, as the bond of Christian unity. Even though they have different gifts, all believers receive the same Spirit. This is what makes them one. So in his benediction Paul is thinking not of a threefold nature in God but of three things he desires for his followers—that they should have right relations with God, with Christ, and with one another. It is significant that Paul mentions Christ first; here we have the clue to the way his thought develops. "May you possess the grace of Christ," Paul is saying (that is, the salvation Christ has brought you), "and the love of God will then be with you, and you will be inwardly united through the Spirit." In other benedictions Paul speaks only of the grace of Christ; in this fuller prayer he draws out all the things he means in the shorter ones. Christ comes from God and works in us by the Spirit, but there is no suggestion of three divine Persons who are yet one.

Connecting the Spirit with God and Christ

The Spirit, however, is always connected in Paul's mind with God and Christ. If we go through all his epistles carefully, we find that wherever he mentions the Spirit, he speaks also of God and of Christ. "Ye are justified in the name of the Lord Jesus, and by the Spirit of our God." "Through [Christ] we both have access by one Spirit unto the Father." "There are diversities of gifts, but the same Spirit. And there are diversities of ministrations, and the same Lord. And there are diversities of workings, but the same God, who worketh all things in all." Paul joins the three names together without any set purpose. Of its own accord one suggests another to him, just as when we speak of the stars, we think also of the sun and the moon.

The other New Testament writers follow the same pattern. Whenever John mentions the Comforter in his Gospel, he mentions also the Father and the Son. The First Epistle of Peter opens with a greeting "to the elect . . . , according to the foreknowledge of God the Father, in sanctification of the Spirit, unto obedience and sprinkling of the blood of Jesus Christ."

We can easily see how the idea of the Trinity arose naturally from men's study of the New Testament. Although the New Testament writers said nothing clearly and definitely about God's threefold nature, yet they seemed everywhere to take it for granted. They always related the action of the Father to the action of the Son and the Spirit.

We can see, also, how men came to think of the Spirit as a Person. In a very real sense all that is done by the mysterious power is personal. Christ comes to us through the Spirit. We have communion with God through the Spirit. We cannot possibly separate the action of the Spirit from that of divine Persons. We have contact with them through the power that speaks for them. Therefore that

50

power must be personal too. If we stop to think of it, our human relationships follow the same pattern. We talk about the influence our parents have had on us. We don't think of it as something different from them, even though they may have died long ago and only their influence remains. That influence is nothing else than the abiding presence of our parents. At a time when we are tempted to go wrong, their influence comes in and keeps us in the straight path. It has this power over us because they themselves are in it. In the same way God is in his Spirit. Christ speaks to us when it speaks.

Men did not need any theological art to discover that the Spirit was a Person and one of three who could not be separated. We all feel this ourselves as soon as we think about what the Spirit does for us. Its voice is the voice of Christ; it supports our weakness with the power of God. Even in our thoughts we cannot separate it from living personality.

Belief in the Trinity helps our daily living

So while the doctrine of the Trinity has no place in the New Testament, it was bound to grow out of the New Testament teaching. Once it was adopted, it became the framework into which all Christian beliefs were fitted.

The doctrine grew mainly from man's desire to declare, beyond all possibility of doubt, the divine nature of Christ. Christ had spoken for God because he was one with God. His action for the good of man had eternal value because

God was acting through him. Religious leaders realized that if men were to have absolute trust in Christ, they must be convinced that in him they had access to God himself, and they were therefore to think of him as part of God's very being.

Some people have thought of the doctrine of the Trinity as mere theory. They say it deals with things we can't possibly understand and that do not touch our actual Christian life. We must agree that both in ancient and in modern times men have discussed the doctrine mostly in words and ideas that we cannot explain definitely. The ordinary man is inclined to feel that he need not waste his time on such deep and difficult questions. Instead he should devote himself to the plain Christian duties he can understand. Certainly he is right. Intellectual riddles are worth very little unless they help us with our great problem of how to live as Christian men and women. But the belief in the Trinity is by its very nature a practical belief. The object of the men who framed it was to make us sure we can depend fully on Christ. Then we will never doubt that his will is God's will, and all he did for us expressed God's love and purpose.

Men have always found that when they leave the belief in the Trinity behind, something vital to them goes out of Christianity. Jesus becomes little more than a noble and respected Teacher, or one among many great leaders we look up to with reverence. They lose the feeling that his word is final and that we must surrender ourselves wholly to him. Christian faith is the complete acceptance of Christ as Lord, and the doctrine of the Trinity safeguards this faith. So the doctrine that three Persons are united in the being of God, which at first sight seems so far from all the practical interests of men, really gives strength to the faith they must have in their daily living.

The doctrine of the Trinity fails in one way

In one respect the doctrine of the Trinity fails to satisfy us. It allows no real place to the Spirit, which remains a kind of shadow cast by the two actual Persons. There seems to be no definite reason why the Spirit should be there at all. Devout Christians are sometimes troubled by a feeling that they neglect the Spirit. They believe passionately in God and Christ, and they declare that this third Person is equal to the others in power and glory. Yet they find themselves praying without any thought of the Spirit.

We cannot help feeling there is something lacking in a doctrine that thus keeps the Spirit from being real to us. For the first believers the Spirit was the one thing they could be certain of. It was present with them. They could see it working and could feel it in their own hearts. The higher world was real to them because the Spirit, which came forth from it, was so real to them they could almost see it. It is strange indeed that the later doctrine should put the Spirit in second place, so that we do not feel sure it really exists.

The fault lies in ourselves

The fault, though, is not in the doctrine but in ourselves. It lies in our failure to understand that the doctrine is something more than a doctrine. A statement may be true and we may fully agree with it, but it means little to us unless it answers our own needs in some way. Shakespeare observes that ideas by themselves cannot do much to help a man:

> O, who can hold a fire in his hand
> By thinking on the frosty Caucasus?

Just thinking of coolness does not bring it to you. Yet by this very method we sometimes try to be religious. Hold the right doctrines; agree to a number of true statements. And by this thinking about the truth we will come somehow to possess it. But this orthodoxy, this following of church creeds, is worth nothing at all by itself. Our beliefs must enter into our life. We must make an actual contact with God before he can help us. We accept the doctrine of the Trinity, thinking it reveals God's nature to us and brings us into fellowship with him, while all it can do, taken only as a doctrine, is to help us in our thinking. We must grasp the truth which the doctrine contains and let that truth help us to know God—at firsthand—for ourselves. Then we can see that the doctrine of the Trinity is much more than a doctrine. And only then can its truth help us in our daily living.

The Spirit is at the root of all truth

Those who framed the doctrine of the Trinity might have done well to begin with the Spirit instead of seeming to bring it in as a sort of afterthought, after they had said what was chiefly in their minds. "I believe in the Spirit"—that is the very base, the very foundation, of religion. In the midst of this earthly scene I am aware of another world that I must live for. I believe in the Spirit because I know it as a fact. Again and again I have felt it touching me—in moments of exaltation or of quiet thought, in strange experiences, in the love that others have shown me and the love I bear for them. If a man has never known those impulses of the Spirit, everything else in religion is a sealed book to him. He cannot realize what it is all about, any more than a blind man can see the lake and the sunset when you tell him they lie before his unseeing eyes. It is the Spirit that gives us the power to understand all higher truth. Only when it touches us do we awaken to the presence of God and respond to the message of Christ. So we must not think that the belief in the Spirit takes second place in our faith. It is at the root of everything. "The natural man," says Paul, "receiveth not the things of the Spirit of God: for they are foolishness unto him: neither can he know them, because they are spiritually discerned." The first thing we must do in religion is to believe in the Spirit. When we have once done that, the Spirit will lead us unto all truth.

We know the Spirit for ourselves

The doctrine of the Trinity, we see, owes all its meaning to that part of it which it seems almost to leave out of sight. We have a statement about the nature of God, but what is that statement based on? How can we know even that God exists? He may exist only in our imagination. He may be just another name for the universe that lies around us. Many people have held these views. Since God is hidden from sight and reason, there seems to be no way to answer them.

But there is one sufficient answer. Though we cannot find God out by searching, *we know the Spirit*. Its coming is a fact we cannot doubt. It speaks to us plainly of a divine power. Not only does it tell us that God exists, but it reveals something of his nature. Wherever men have believed in God, they have thought of him as holy and just and good—not only because they wish to think of him that way, but because they must. The Spirit compels them to think of God in that way and no other.

The Spirit also assures us of the relation of Christ to God. The idea that God was revealed in Christ might seem to be utterly without foundation. Many men have tried to show that this idea was nothing but a myth or superstition. They said it arose, like many others, in an ignorant age. But there is sure evidence for this idea. The early disciples believed it because they witnessed the works of the Spirit with their own eyes. We believe it still because we have fellowship with Christ through the Spirit. We find that his will is God's will. The more we grow like him, the more we enter into the divine life.

Even as the Spirit testifies to some inward relation between Christ and God, so it also testifies to itself. When it enters into us, we know that this is something out of a higher world. This power that guides us and sustains us and enlightens us is one with God and with Christ, who revealed him. In a real sense the doctrine of the Trinity is necessary to our Christian faith. It sums up the truths which pervade all the New Testament teaching, though it may not be stated openly there. It is proved also by our own deepest experience of God and of the Spirit and of Christ. We know them as three and yet as one.

Still the doctrine of the Trinity helps us only when we look beyond its literal sense. It was drawn up in an age when men tried to state their beliefs in terms of reason, and this can never be done. We cannot explain faith or love by a mathematical formula, as we can a law of matter. Those higher things, we say, are spiritual. We must feel them inwardly before we can understand them. This is supremely true when we try to express the nature of God. Many good Christians cannot accept the doctrine of the Trinity as it is set forth in the creed, yet they believe in it. They never doubt that God is over all, that he has revealed himself in Christ, that he comes to us in the power of his Spirit. They know that God and Christ and the Spirit cannot be separated and are one God.

The words of the doctrine do not greatly matter as long as we grasp their essential meaning. Indeed, one of the functions of the Spirit is just this—to take old forms and doctrines and help us so to understand them that they will have a vital meaning to us. We do not really believe until we can state the old truth in our own way and still find it true.

CHAPTER FOUR

THE SPIRIT'S RELATION TO MAN

ALL THROUGH THE BIBLE, IN BOTH THE OLD TESTA-
ment and the New Testament, the writers connect the
Holy Spirit with human life. We might have expected that
early men would be most impressed by strange events in
the world of nature and see the Spirit at work in storms
and eclipses and volcanoes. These do indeed have a great
place in old religions, but they are not usually credited to
the Spirit. Early men thought of the Spirit as a power that
reveals itself in the lives of men. No doubt a few Old
Testament writers, especially the author of the story of the
creation, thought of it in a more general way, but the main
interest of even these writers is human. The Spirit is life-
giving. All things that live have that much in common
with men—the Spirit has breathed into them an element
of a higher kind.

The Spirit sets man apart from other creatures

It is very remarkable that even the most primitive men
could see the difference between human beings and the
world around them. Early men noticed that things without
life were subject to fixed laws. They could tell exactly how

59

fire and wind and water would act, and so could use care in dealing with them. Birds and animals were living creatures, able to move freely, but they never went beyond their limits. They could be counted on to act in a certain way under each given set of circumstances.

But with men it was different. Men did have regular habits and customs, it is true, but from time to time sudden impulses moved them. Those impulses could not be foretold and did not seem to be their own. So early men recognized that while they belonged to this world, they were somehow connected with another. They were not bound by those laws that rule all other creatures. Man was a being by himself, allied to an order of things that had nothing to do with the world he saw. Every now and then he was forced to act in a strange way, moved by some power outside the known order of things. From the first, men saw this as the thing that set them apart from the rest of creation. The Spirit, they saw, comes only to man. And man alone is able to respond to the Spirit.

In early times men did not try to explain this fact. They were content on the whole to take their place with the other animals. Often they had to struggle against those animals to stay alive. In many ways they felt the animals were superior to themselves. Many of these early people believed that the souls of men and beasts kept changing back and forth, so that after death a man might be reborn as a beast and a beast as a man. Yet no one ever doubted that man was the only creature who could be touched by this mysterious power outside the known order of things. This was what made him human.

Thinkers in all times have been trying to lay a finger on the thing in man that makes him by his very nature different from other creatures. Different ones have pointed to different things: his gift of reason, his use of language, his ability to make tools or to combine in social groups. But other animals can do all these things in some crude way, and the lowest types of savage men often show little trace of them. We must go back to the idea that the earliest people reached by instinct—man is man because he is in contact with a higher world. He has the power to worship. He can receive messages that come to him from the Spirit.

Man has an affinity to the Spirit

So the Spirit is related to God and brings man something of God's nature. But it is related also to man. Man could not answer to the Spirit unless he had within himself some affinity to the Spirit—unless there was between God and man a natural attraction of like to like. Man sees and hears because his eyes and ears are so made that they respond to light and sound. Man knows the Spirit for himself because something within him is so made that it responds to the Spirit.

Man belongs to this world. He is subject to all its laws. Hunger and thirst affect him as they do all other animals. When a roof falls down on him, it crushes him just as it crushes the chair he may be sitting on. Yet he also belongs to a world where the physical laws do not matter. He has a spiritual nature that is ruled only by the forces of truth and love and honor and justice. When all is said, this is the great difference between man and every other creature we know: though he lives in this world, man is linked with that higher world from which the Spirit comes.

The Spirit awakens man to his true nature

The work of the Spirit is to awaken man to a sense of his true nature. We read of men in the old times who were captured by the Indians and lived with them for years as members of the tribe. They forgot everything they had been before. Then one day they heard someone speak their native tongue, and everything came back to them. They knew their home was somewhere else. They realized that in the forest they were strangers and captives. That is what happens to a man who hears the voice of the Spirit. It may seem to come to him for the first time, but it strikes a familiar note. It reminds him of what he is. It brings back to him a life he has been separated from.

Paul has much to say about the gifts of the Spirit. He seems to think they are gifts that create in man abilities he never had before. A quite ordinary man became all at once an eloquent speaker, or he showed a courage or an insight that seemed miraculous. The Spirit had given him powers he had never even dreamed of having. But this, we can be sure, was only half the truth. The man who surprised everyone by his eloquence must have had that gift already without knowing it. The man or woman who performed beautiful deeds of mercy must have had a generous soul that had never before found full expression. The Spirit did not work by magic. In every case it found something that it could mold and develop so as to bring forth the new and better things.

So it was in the early Church, and so it has always been. John Milton asks for the aid of the Spirit at the beginning of his great poem *Paradise Lost,* but it could have done little for him if he had not possessed the genius of a poet. John Wesley said the success of his work was due to the Spirit. And he was right. But we must remember that Wesley was a born leader of men and that the Spirit used him because he was fitted above all others to be its instrument.

As it is with the special gifts, so it is with the very capacity of men to receive the Spirit. It is not something from outside their nature that is poured in. It is something inside themselves that is related to the Spirit and can respond to it when it comes.

The Spirit helps man use the gifts he has

We might say that the Spirit gives man nothing new. Its work is rather to make him aware of the gifts he already has. For one thing, it rouses him to the sense that he has a higher nature which has lain buried under all his concern with this passing life. This is always the first effect of the Spirit when it touches a man. The man discovers, often with amazement, that he has a soul. He cries out like the Philippian jailer in a sudden crisis, "What shall I do to be saved?" When a man is thus awakened, his interests become entirely different. But he knows that these have always been his true interests, even if he has given no heed to them before.

Again, the Spirit brings with it a new power of vision. We are like a nearsighted man who has found the right glasses. He looks out on the familiar scene, but everything in it is changed. There is beauty where he never guessed it before. He sees men and things as they really are. He no longer stumbles among shadows.

The Bible has much to say about the wisdom given by the Spirit. It speaks of the falling of scales from the eyes. The spiritual man looks at the facts before him, and he sees them clearly without prejudice or illusion. His decisions are the right ones, for he is able to use his eyes. We have all found in our own experience that the counsel of a good Christian man is usually the best, even in matters of common business. "He that is spiritual," says Paul, "judgeth all things."

While the Spirit may give us nothing new, it gives strength and direction to all the powers we have. It is comforting to think that all of us have reserves of strength we don't know about. Frail women in the stress of a great emergency have endured hardships and overcome difficulties that would have terrified the strongest men. This same power is hidden away somewhere in all of us. The

Spirit helps us to reach down to it. The Spirit comes to our aid, but it acts in the main to show us what we can do ourselves. We can stand up to what seems impossible —that has always been the message of the Spirit. It has inspired all the noblest deeds that men have ever done.

Man's spirit bears witness with the Spirit

The Spirit thus makes its appeal to man's own nature. It comes from God, but there is something in man that knows and answers it. This is the evidence that in his inner being man belongs to God. It is also the evidence that man's belief in God and in a higher world is true.

Someone is always asking the question, "How can you prove your religion?" It tells you of things that are beautiful and tempting, but how can you know they are anything but wishful thinking? The New Testament offers many answers to this question, but they all go back to this one answer: in our inmost nature we feel the truth of the Christian message. The Spirit bears witness with our spirits. In other words, the message comes to us, and we find it is in harmony with everything that is best in ourselves.

Take, for instance, the Beatitudes. If Jesus had said, "Blessed are the proud, the self-satisfied, the rich and successful," many people would no doubt have agreed with him. He would have stated the view of life most people live by. But even the most worldly man knows in his heart that it is a false and ignoble view. Jesus put it aside and said, "Blessed are the meek, the poor, those who suffer for a good cause." And we know he was right. We know it because something in us tells us so. We may argue as we please on the other side, and many of the cleverest men will support us. But all the time we know it is wrong. Our own spirit bears witness that Jesus spoke the truth.

The New Testament makes this the test of all we must believe: Does the thing the Spirit tells us find an echo in our own inner self? Then we have a witness to it. And it is the only witness we can depend on completely. The one thing we can come nearest to being sure of is our own being. And that being is in harmony at its very center with the truth as Christ revealed it.

The Spirit proves to man the truth of the gospel

This idea of the witness of the Spirit is expressed most clearly in the First Epistle of John. John writes to a group of Christians who have begun to doubt their faith. Like many people today, they have been confused by some highly intellectual teachers. These teachers said the gospel as they had learned it was out of date. They said it did not produce the true life. John offers these Christians certain tests by which they can tell if this true life is in them. Can they resist evil in all its forms? Do they love one another? Above all, has the Spirit said to them just what their own hearts would say at the times when they truly understood themselves? This for John is the decisive

THE SPIRIT'S RELATION TO MAN

proof that clinches the truth of the gospel. The gospel has
not come as something which is entirely new and which
therefore can be argued over. Christ has only declared
plainly what men have always known in their inmost being
to be true. The Spirit has spoken through him. It also
speaks within us, and the two voices are in full agreement.
We believe the gospel in the last analysis because it answers so perfectly to the witness within us.

Men have tried in countless ways to prove the Christian
message. Whole libraries of the most scholarly books have
been written for this one purpose. But none of them
satisfies us. We always feel that the argument which helps
to prove one side might be turned around and used to
prove just the opposite. The one proof we must always
fall back on is the evidence of the Spirit.

In an important trial there may be dozens of witnesses,
who all have something to say for one side or the other.
But everything might hinge on the evidence of one man
who can say definitely, "I saw the thing happen." So in
the trial of Christianity, which is always going on, no one
can really refute the evidence of the Spirit. The Spirit
knows the mind of God and tells us clearly that the message we believe in has come from him.

In one way, though, the Spirit not only proves the
truth of what we already know but also tells us things that
are new. John says in his Gospel, "The Spirit was not
yet given; because Jesus was not yet glorified." Here John
contradicts himself. He has taken it for granted elsewhere

67

that the Spirit has always been active and that all the work of Jesus was done in the power of the Spirit. Yet he can truly say that the Spirit as we now know it did not appear until after Jesus had departed, for Jesus gave the Spirit a meaning it had not had before. He made it richer with his own personality, with his own condition of mind. The Spirit as he gave it was like light that has passed through a stained-glass window. It is in essence the same light, but the stained glass gives it a new rich color. The Spirit is now so identified with Christ himself that we cannot separate it from him. Paul and John in their writings often speak in the same sentence of Christ and the Spirit. Sometimes they weave the two ideas together in the phrase "the Spirit of Christ," which we still use all the time.

So we have a simple test by which we can tell if we have really received the Spirit. The early Christians often found this a serious difficulty. A man would appear who was plainly filled with enthusiasm. He would talk in exalted language and see visions. How could they be sure he was not just a fanatic? How could they tell that the Spirit was really speaking through him? They could be sure only by comparing his words with those of Jesus to see if they agreed. John warns his followers, "Believe not every spirit, but try the spirits whether they are of God." And Paul says emphatically, "If any man have not the Spirit of Christ, he is none of his." We need these warnings to-day.

Every now and then some movement starts up that

claims to be Christian. Perhaps it is connected with opinions and practices strange to us, but we must not condemn it for that reason. Many times the best of men have been martyred because they did not serve God in just the approved way. But we have the right to ask certain things of every new movement. Is it really in harmony with the teaching of Christ? Do those who follow it live as he did? Are they inspired with his faith in God and his love of his fellow men? If they are, we must not laugh at them or turn them away, no matter how strange their behavior may seem to us. The Spirit has touched them; they are acting sincerely by its guidance. We cannot deny them the name of Christian unless there is something in their beliefs that is clearly opposed to the mind of Christ.

How can man get the Spirit for himself?

We find the answer to another difficult question when we think of the Spirit as we know it through Christ. It is the power that strengthens and illuminates—but how can we get it for ourselves? Sometimes it seems to come all by itself by some happy accident we cannot explain.

Darwin tells us that for some years he had been working on his great theory; he had made himself ill in the vain effort to discover the principle that would make it practical. Then one day he stepped into his carriage, thinking only of the pleasant drive before him. While he raised his foot from the ground, the idea of natural selection flashed into his mind. Similar moments have come in the lives of all great poets and artists and discoverers. They can do nothing without that sudden inspiration, but they can only wait till it pleases to come.

Men have tried many methods of compelling the Spirit, especially in religion. Sometimes their plan is to collect people together and stir them up into a mass excitement. Sometimes it is rather to withdraw them into a place of peace and privacy where they may fast and meditate and so persuade the Spirit to come in. No one can say these attempts are futile. Favorable conditions are always necessary if anything great is to happen. We can at least prepare the way for the Spirit. Yet we must never forget that all we do is only a *preparation*. The Spirit comes always of its own accord. It will not be forced.

There is one way, however, by which we can make sure of obtaining the Spirit. The Spirit became one with Christ, and through him it was given to his disciples. In so far as we believe in him and do his commandments, to that extent shall we receive the Spirit that dwelt in him.

The New Testament teaching joins faith and the Spirit together, so much so that the rite of baptism, in which a man declares his faith in Christ, is supposed to carry with it the gift of the Spirit. The belief opened the door to many ideas that were more pagan than Christian. It let men ascribe a mysterious quality to the water of baptism. They believed it carried the Spirit by some magical process and changed the nature of those who were washed in it. Paul is always careful to make it clear that the thing that counts in baptism is faith. The outward rite serves only to put a seal on our surrender to Christ. That surrender, or faith, makes it possible for him to give us his Spirit. Early Christians acknowledged this fully, and the Baptists in our own day have done a great service in keeping us mindful of it.

But whatever value baptism may have, we ought not to think of it as more than a beginning. The receiving of the Spirit is not so much a single act as the work of a lifetime. If we accept Christ as our Master, we set ourselves to follow him. We believe what he has taught us about God. We try to perform all duties as he would have us do. We try to mold our character according to his pattern. By this obedience to Christ we receive the Spirit that was his, just as a plant absorbs the life-giving essence of the soil.

Thus we can receive the Spirit without knowing it, just by living the Christian life. No doubt the Spirit comes sometimes in a single burst—everyone can look back on special times when he was lifted above his ordinary self and felt the impulse of a higher power. But most often the Spirit comes quietly as we carry out our everyday duties and seek to do them faithfully according to the will of Christ.

Many men and women will tell you sadly that they have never enjoyed those high experiences that have come to others, to whom God has clearly given his Spirit. Their lives have been dull and ordinary. When they read of the great saints, they doubt if they can truly call themselves Christians. Yet perhaps it is these people who most truly possess the Spirit. It has come to them so gradually that they have scarcely been aware of it. They think it is not there because it is with them so constantly they take it for granted. "Now the Lord is that Spirit," says Paul. Those who follow the Lord may be sure the Spirit is with them.

CHAPTER FIVE

WE NEED THE SPIRIT TODAY

I CANNOT STRESS THIS FACT TOO MUCH: BELIEF IN THE Holy Spirit grows out of a real experience. We have come too much to think that belief in the Spirit is a sort of fiction of religion. For some reason, we think, the early Christians assumed there was a mysterious power working along with God and Christ. So they framed the doctrine of the Trinity, a doctrine that still holds a place in our creeds. But the doctrine has little meaning for us today. It is simply a group of words we repeat without thinking. In this practical age, when we care only for things that are real, we have quietly dropped it as a living part of our religion.

But the truth is that men believed in the Spirit because it was a fact that forced itself on their minds. At a time when they had no clear sense of God, they still were conscious of this power, which they called the Spirit. They could not help knowing that it existed, for they saw it acting on men who did marvelous things. They felt its impulses ever and again in their own lives. The early Christians did not invent the Spirit. They heard it coming on them, we are told, as a mighty rushing wind, which filled the place where they were met together. They knew they had received new energies, which must have come to them from above. They went out on a world-wide mission and found that this new power supported and guided them in their mission. When they framed their belief in the Spirit, they were not just putting into words some abstract thinking. They were trying to explain visible facts which they could not account for in any other way.

We have forgotten the Spirit

Robert Louis Stevenson tells us in one of his essays that when he was a boy, he sailed out for some miles to see the founding of a lighthouse. Nothing would satisfy him but to put on the diving suit and go down fathoms deep with the diver. When they stood on the floor of the sea, his companion signaled to him to spring onto a great rock which towered high above his head. Young Stevenson thought the man was joking, but the man repeated the signal. Stevenson made the spring and felt himself lifted up till he stood on the rock. He had forgotten that the water was a buoyant element—that a force in the ocean would support his tiny effort and bear him up.

Just as truly, there is a spiritual force that supports and enlarges our own feeble efforts. We forget about it. We let ourselves be frightened by all the things that stand in our way. But we must trust this force, and it will not fail us. This is the truth the first disciples came to know after the Lord's departure. It holds good now as it did then.

Perhaps our chief need in these modern days is to recover the old belief in the Spirit. We try to do everything ourselves, and we accomplish very little, yet all the time that other power is waiting to help us.

We often speak of the need for a religious revival, as if only our churches suffered from a decay of the old energy. But we can easily trace the same symptoms everywhere. Wherever we look, we can find able men doing good work, but we miss all signs of inspiration. We have no great art or literature. Our statesmen and leaders are content merely to keep things going, with very poor success even at that. No one has much enthusiasm about anything. Men work only for pay and then with the one desire to do as little as possible. Sometimes it happens that a river dries up or finds a channel underground, and as a result a once fruitful country turns into a desert. A change of this kind seems to have overtaken whole regions of our life today.

We think too much of material things

One reason we live today in a desert of the spirit is that our minds have been so busy with material things. We are justly proud of all we have learned during the last hundred years. We have learned many things about the laws of nature. We have built machines that are almost unbelievable. We have learned to use the earth's resources and to pile up wealth at a rate never dreamed of in days gone by. Our ability to do all this has whetted our desire, and our minds look forward to little else than to add to our possessions and get new means of physical comfort.

But as we have learned more we have come to realize how vast the material world is and how tiny is our own place in it. Infinite spaces and incalculable forces are all around us. We feel ourselves utterly crushed by them. How can we dare to put any value on our little human lives? What are we but the merest specks on this earth? And what is the earth itself but a grain of sand on the shores of an endless universe? The new things we have learned have indeed given us the key to unlock many secrets, but they have won their triumphs at a heavy cost. They have taught us to feel that while we have done so much, we ourselves are nothing. The wonders we have discovered have been too much for us. They have made our old hopes and dreams seem silly. It is not surprising that men have come to think chiefly about material things, for the awe they once directed toward spiritual things is now turned toward the things they can see. And those things have proved to be so stupendous they can think of nothing beyond them.

But may there not be a world that is different in kind from this one, a world where material things count for nothing? Pascal, the seventeenth-century French philosopher and mathematician, was one of the fathers of modern science. In a famous passage he confessed that when he thought of the universe in its vastness, he was terrified. What was he but a straw or an atom? But, he goes on to say, he also felt that he was greater than the universe. The universe did not know that it existed, while he could think about the universe and could aspire to something beyond it. This is indeed the faith with which we may face the whole material world. Although the universe has no limits, yet it is nothing but matter, while man has something in him that belongs to another order altogether. Man feels this when he reflects on his own nature. What he feels is proved to him by the Spirit, which comes out of that higher world.

Paul speaks of the Spirit as an "earnest"—a first installment which guarantees the whole payment that lies in store for us. An impulse of the Spirit is our security for a whole spiritual world—the world from which we derive our being and which we can live for while we are still confined to this earth.

We think we can stand alone

We have grown to forget the Spirit because in this age we are weighted down with a sense of how vast the material world is. And there is still another reason why we forget the Spirit. Men have done so much that they have come to have an overweening confidence in themselves. They imagine they can do everything. We can hardly open a book without meeting some scornful remark about the simple faith of our fathers. According to these remarks, our fathers expected that God would do all things for them. Therefore they never roused themselves to find cures for sickness, to improve ways of travel, to make use of precious material lying at their feet, to set up systems of government that would be just and reasonable. So say these modern writers.

The truth is that with their smaller knowledge our forefathers did a great deal, though we assume they did nothing. We think we are the first to discover that God helps those who help themselves. Indeed, we even say he does not help us at all. He has given us hands and minds; he requires only that we use them and do our own work as we think best.

The book of Acts tells us that Paul asked a group of people if they had received the Holy Spirit. They answered, "We have not so much as heard whether there be any Holy Ghost." Many people today feel the same way. They are so sure they must do everything by themselves that they never even think of the Spirit. If any whisper from the Spirit ever comes to them, they put it aside and insist that everything must be of their own making. Before they do anything, they collect the facts and balance them against one another. Then they decide by their own judgment what course will bring the most profit. The one thing they try to avoid is to yield to any mere impulse, no matter what kind of impulse it is. For a long time past, men have counted this the only kind of wisdom. They have been trying to mold the world according to their own plans entirely. They act as if they never even heard there is a Holy Spirit.

Can we say that modern men have much reason to be proud of what they have accomplished? For a whole generation they have been tearing one another in pieces. They have turned much of the earth into a wilderness. They have thrown into utter confusion all that man has achieved by centuries of patient labor. When we look at the deeper causes, we see that this has all come about because men were so determined to shape the world by themselves. They would not believe that any higher power had a hand in it. They pulled everything down so they could build it over according to their own wisdom. Now that everything lies in ruins, they still cry for more planning, more tricks of policy, more organization. Men have blundered, yes. So they must begin all over again—and repeat the same mistakes in some different way.

Our bitter experience has gone for little if it has not taught us that man cannot do everything by himself. He must wait on a power that works along with him. He must act at times on impulses that come to him, he cannot tell how. They move him to do things that seem foolish by all standards of this world. The mind of our age is all for planning in advance, but in our anxiety to plan every step before we take it, we leave one thing out—the most important thing.

Sometimes we hear about a miser who has dragged out his life in poverty, spending only a few pennies a day, while all the time he had abundant wealth on which he would never draw. Many, many people today are doing the same thing. They want to do everything out of their own poor resources, though they have access to a divine power they never draw upon.

The Spirit gives us daring

A sense of this divine power upon which we can draw would make us able, for one thing, to venture—and without venture we can never achieve great things. We can do nothing, even in matters of common business, without some element of risk, for nothing in this world is certain. Our life consists in a steady going forward into a country we do not know. As each day begins, we can only guess how it will end. We are all pioneers, traveling on without a map to guide us. Yet we shut our eyes to this fact, the condition on which our lives are given us.

We try to work out ways to make everything secure. No doubt within certain limits we need to do this. A wise man provides for his old age and insures his house against fire. He sees to it that someone bridges and fences dangerous places. Yet we can never be secure. Perhaps our chief error in these days is our wish to have all the good of life without the dangers. We resent those dangers as if they had no right to be there. We keep away from all duties and opportunities until we are sure we will be safe.

This is a foolish habit of mind. It saps our strength and keeps us dull and miserable. For when all is said, risk is a necessary part of life, and without it life loses all its zest. This wish to be secure weakens us even for our daily work. But most of all it weakens us for the really great tasks. Here we know the job is hard. We can see plainly that the odds are all against us. We begin to measure our own ability against the huge obstacle we will have to overcome. So we decide the thing cannot be done, and we need not try it.

There are evils today we all admit are terrible, but no one lifts a finger to correct them. The wrong has such deep roots, it is backed by such mighty forces, that we feel we must leave it standing. So we go round it as best we can. Yet in times past there have been evils just as great, that seemed just as hard to overcome. But someone ventured to do the thing that could not be done—and did it. For instance, there was that little group of humble Christians who matched themselves against the Roman Empire. Men laughed at them and called them crazy fanatics. They had a hard struggle, but they made the tremendous venture and won.

The New Testament tells us how those early believers were able to do the impossible. They felt a power behind them which would support their feeble effort, as the force of the ocean lifted up the boy when he dared to make his spring. In our day men study the size of a task before them and tell us it cannot be done. Since they depend only on themselves, we cannot blame them for holding back. But if they trusted the Spirit, they would at least make the venture. They would find they received a strength that is not of this world, a strength no earthly force can withstand.

The time we live in has added many new articles to our creed, and for most men these new articles have taken the place of the old ones. "I believe in progress." "I believe in science." "I believe in the wisdom of the people." These may all be sound beliefs, but none of them will help us much if we give up that ancient one, "I believe in the Holy Spirit." We may think it has become an abstract thought without meaning for us, but it is still the vital spring of all that is greatest in human life.

The Spirit gives us freedom

Besides giving us the daring to throw ourselves into tasks that seem utterly beyond us, the Spirit also gives us a sense of freedom—which we need more than anything else in our time. We have come to think of freedom as something we have inherited. Or we think of it as something that comes from just laws and wealth and military power. But freedom must not be confused with any outward conditions.

Freedom, as we have seen, is the inward faith that your soul is your own, the faith that you are responsible in the last resort to God alone. The men who stand out in history as the grand examples of free men lived for the most part under oppression. Many of them spent much of their lives in prison. It was when they were in chains that they were most proudly conscious that they were free. The tyrant might do his worst; they could rely on something in them that he could never hold down. This is the only true freedom, and it is given by the Spirit. The Spirit speaks to us of God; it tells us we belong to him and can submit to no other. Once we possess this inward freedom, we are sure to win, sooner or later, every other kind of freedom.

The chief danger that threatens us in this age is the danger of losing our freedom. We fought a great war to set enslaved people free. In the course of it we learned with a shock that many of these people did not want to be free. If they were only left in peace with enough to live on, they were content to serve under any master. Great numbers of people think this same way today, even when they shout most loudly that they must have liberty. What they really want is safety and comfort, perhaps at the expense of others. If they can have these things, they are willing to put up with any conditions. The mass of people do not really want to be free. That is the main reason why we are in danger of losing our freedom.

No age before this has ever offered such opportunities to dictators and to movements whose deliberate aim is to do away with all individual rights. The reason can only be that our sense of the importance of persons is growing weaker. Men have come to think of themselves as on the same level as bees and ants. They are willing to be organized in much the same way. They give up their souls because they do not seriously believe they have any. When this is their state of mind, freedom cannot possibly have any meaning to them.

There are many who tell us lightly, and even boastfully, that they have no religion. They take it for granted that this makes little difference for any practical purpose. They can do their work and be good citizens and good friends just as well as if they were religious men. But it does make a profound difference in all they do and all they are, for religion gives man a sense of God. Because of that the religious man has an inner freedom, so he faces everything in life as a free man.

So we can almost see freedom losing ground. It is slipping away from us, not because of any outside force, but because of a change in our own minds. We have let our faith in God grow weaker and weaker, and with it goes our own dignity as human beings. All our liberties are bound up with this faith, in the last resort.

The great question is now being decided—will men survive as free persons, each with his separate value, or only as fragments in a general mass of humanity? Will life be worth having if there is no freedom, no responsibility? If we are not to be ourselves, why should we have come into this world at all?

We need a new impulse of the Spirit

What we need in this momentous age is a new impulse of the Spirit. Deep down in the hearts of all of us is the sense of a higher world, the world we are meant to live for. How can we awaken and keep alive this sense of our calling? Only by a power from above to which our own souls can respond.

When the Spirit touches a man, he becomes aware that he himself is a spiritual being. And he realizes that he can find his true life only when he resists all forces that would take away his self-respect and make him a slave. Our eyes have been opened in our time to many pressing needs, and we do right to honor those who are trying to supply them. We need better education. We need more money for more people. We need better understanding among men and nations. But above all else we need a new breath of the Spirit. The other things would all come if we had that.

Once more, we need the Spirit to wake up our sense of the moral principles on which all human action must be founded. "He that is spiritual," says Paul, "judgeth all things." He is able to measure them by eternal standards of right and wrong. For this purpose the Spirit came upon the prophets. They spoke to the nation when it had to make momentous choices. They did not ask themselves which course would give them the greatest advantage. They thought only of what was morally right. This was all God cared for, and they declared his mind as it was revealed to them.

In our own troubles we pray for the Spirit to guide us. If our prayer is sincere, it is always answered. We may not learn exactly what we should do, but our minds are cleared of all pretenses and selfish motives. We are made to realize, as we pray, that we must look first to what is just and honorable and kind. We have asked the Spirit to guide us; it has never yet advised any man to do what was morally wrong.

Now in our time men usually worry about the moral issues last. There is endless political discussion, but it all turns on what will be best for our material interests. The man who brings up some purely moral question is brushed aside as an idealist who ought not to meddle in practical affairs. So in the conduct of our daily lives we draw a line between action and strict morality. We may do things in business that do not quite follow the Ten Commandments. We may choose people as our friends even though we know their characters would not stand a close inspection. So in every way the idea that all things must be judged by moral standards is dying out of our modern life.

Someone asked a wise man several years ago what he thought was the root cause of all the present confusion. He answered, "The want of common honesty." We cannot help feeling that he came very near the truth. For a long time now everyone has been running loose, acting as he pleased without any regard to eternal principles of right. The result has been much the same as if the law of gravitation were suddenly to stop operating. We seem to have forgotten that men did not make the moral principles, leaving themselves free to change them or throw them away as they wished. God established them. And when men pay no attention to them, all human society falls to pieces. Most often we are reminded of them too late by the dismal results of what we have done. But God warns us in advance by his Spirit. He seeks to keep us in the right way.

What we need most today is to have the old simple rules of duty and truth and loyalty and human kindness so impressed on us that we can never doubt them. Unless a new moral enthusiasm takes over in our lives, all we have done and all we know will help us little.

How can we find the Spirit?

How can we get this impulse of the Spirit? Sometimes it comes suddenly and miraculously. A mysterious power takes hold of a man and changes him all at once into a new man. A passion for righteousness sweeps over a nation like a forest fire. This is what we usually think of when we speak of a revival, and no doubt the Spirit sometimes acts in this manner.

Perhaps in our modern religion we are much too formal and self-contained. Perhaps those sects that shock us at times by their great display of emotion are doing us a very real service. They remind us that there is such a thing as ecstasy. Ancient people thought of it as the central thing, and so did the early Christians. And we must always allow a place for it.

The Spirit may rush upon a man like a gust of wind and lift him completely out of himself. Yet it may also come quietly. Too often we fold our hands and hope for a revival when we ourselves might be helping it come. The earth is kept fruitful, not by floods that burst in from time to time, but by gentle rain that is constantly falling. A thousand people meet together and pray for a new day of Pentecost, and they feel all the time that there is little sign of it. But if in their separate lives they were all to do the will of Christ, in whom the Spirit was manifested, the Pentecost would come. When the quiet acts of a thousand devoted Christian people are all put together, they make up a great outpouring of the Spirit. It is this combined influence of many lives, no one of them very important in itself but each inspired by Christ, that will bring revival to the world.

One thing we must always remember—the belief in the Holy Spirit rests upon a *fact*. From the very first, men ever and again felt impulses from above that awakened something divine in them. They were conscious of a power sent forth from God to keep them in touch with him and to remind them that in this earthly life they were still his children. When Christ appeared, they knew his message was true because it answered to the message of the Spirit. So when we say, "I believe in the Spirit," we declare our faith in a higher world, in our own spiritual nature, in all that Christ has taught us about God. We believe these things, not because of what others say, but because of what we ourselves know. The Spirit has come to us in moments of high experience or of silent thought, and we cannot doubt its witness. If we believe in the Spirit and follow its guidance, it will lead us unto all truth.

NOTES

Page	Line	
48	4	Matt. 28:19
48	19	II Cor. 13:14
49	24	I Cor. 6:11
49	26	Eph. 2:18
50	1	I Cor. 12:4-6 (A.S.V.)
50	11	I Pet. 1:1-2 (A.S.V.)
55	22	I Cor. 2:14
64	20	I Cor. 2:15
65	18	Paraphrase of Rom. 8:16
67	26	John 7:39 (A.S.V.)
68	23	I John 4:1
68	25	Rom. 8:9
72	5	II Cor. 3:17
78	14	Acts 19:2
85	18	I Cor. 2:15